WORKBOOK FOR

YOU'RE GOING TO MAKE IT

(A Guide to Lysa Terkeurst's Book)

Your Powerful Guide on Imbibing Lifestyle that Unrush Your Mind, Uncomplicate your Heart and Bring Healing Today

ALL RIGHTS RESERVED…

THIS ONE WEEK OUTLINE WAS DEVELOPED TO HELP YOU.

> The foremost thing
is to find a
person you can rely on to
 help you achieve your
goals if you want to be
successful.

> Be careful not
to make any mistakes
when filling out the vital
forms displayed below.

> Consider each day's tip,
task and prescription
carefully.

**THINK ABOUT THEM
MEDITATIVELY.**

➢ **Everything you learned in the note should be written and meditated upon.**

Also, jot down your thoughts and feelings, as well as the obstacles you've come to terms with.

READ AND LISTEN TO
EVERYTHING
THAT IS BEING SAID
AND RECOMMENDED.

Without a doubt, adhere to
them.

**IT WAS MADE TO BE
POSSIBLE.**

Never doubt the fact that
you
can do it, and never give up
hope.

**YOU'RE ALL SET TO STEP
ON TO THE NEXT LEVEL!**

Ensure that you fill out the Form below in its entirety.

DATE IT ALL BEGINS

_____

_____

DATE OF FINAL CONCLUSION (Usually 7 Days from the starting Date)

_____

Fill in the blanks with your name and email address:

_____

_____

FILL OUT YOUR AGE

_____

_____

It's not as difficult as you might
think, but don't take it for
granted and keep going.

Recommendations and
Tasks for the Day Don't End
That Day; Carry On and
Make Habits of Them.

DAY 1

INSIGHT

Learn how to pour out all your troubles and sorrow before almighty God, knowing that he is God and has the power to heal you of your grievances and pain.

WHAT YOU SHOULD IMBIBE TODAY

Pray fervently to God for whatever it is that is stealing your peace. Ask him to come to your aid and heal you of your troubles.

<u>DON'T FORGET...</u>

When you pray to God, remove doubt, knowing that you are talking to the Lord of host and King of Kings.

MEDITATE

_____

_____

_____

_____

_____

_____

_____

_____

_____

_____

_____

_____

_____

_____

_____

_____

_____

_____

_____

_____

_____

_____

_____

_____

_____

_____

_____

_____

Don't doubt the power of the most High God, don't hide anything from him or feel your need is much.

DAY 2

INSIGHT

Accepting the things you can't change or control is one of the greatest ways of attaining peace and happiness in life.

WHAT YOU SHOULD IMBIBE TODAY...

Stop fighting those things that are bigger and stronger than you, ignore them and build yourself. Doing this on its own makes you the boss over them.

DON'T FORGET...

You give things power you when you
pay attention to them!!!

MEDITATE

_____

_____

_____

_____

_____

_____

_____

_____

_____

_____

_____

_____

_____

_____

_____

_____

_____

_____

_____

_____

_____

_____

_____

_____

_____

**Ignore hate and losers,
that's the much they can do
with their wretched lives.**

DAY 3

INSIGHT

Forgiving your offenders of the ills they did against you has more positive impact in your life than you ever imagine. It brings you peace, happiness, mental clarity, grace and more.

WHAT YOU SHOULD IMBIBE TODAY

Ponder on all the people that have done you bad in the past, commit their evils into God's hands, forgive them, forget them and move on with your life and personal effort for growth.

18

DON'T FORGET...

To err is human but to forgive is divine!!!!

MEDITATE...

_____

_____
_____
_____
_____
_____
_____
_____
_____
_____
_____
_____

**Letting go of people's
wrongdoings opens greater
doors in your life.**
_____

DAY 4

INSIGHT

Proper meditation takes you far away from the thieves of your peace; it opens your mind to proper decisions that make your life better.

WHAT YOU SHOULD IMBIBE TODAY

In a quiet place, sit calmly and meditate on life. Think on your problems and how to solve them.

DON'T FORGET...

Proper meditation opens your mind up
to unseen reality.

MEDITATE

_____

_____

_____

_____

_____

_____

_____

_____

_____

_____

_____

_____

_____

_____

_____

_____

_____

_____

_____

_____

_____

_____

_____

_____

_____

_____

_____

In each day that passes, think about your life!!!

DAY 5

INSIGHT

No matter how busy you think you are in this world, making out time for yourself would always be more beneficial. Find yourself and your peace in this frantic world.

WHAT YOU SHOULD IMBIBE TODAY...

Force out time for yourself today. Sit back on your own and discover the places you're lacking. Solve your problems from now.

DON'T FORGET

If you over stress and die, the world
will still move on!!!

MEDITATE

_____

_____

_____

_____

_____

_____

_____

_____

_____

_____

_____

_____

_____

_____

_____

_____

_____

_____

_____

_____

_____

_____

_____

_____

_____

Don't let the pursuit of anybody drain you of your energy, it's not worth it.

DAY 6

INSIGHT

Visualize your dream life and happy place, knowing and believing that you'd get there sooner than later.

WHAT YOU SHOULD IMBIBE TODAY

As you work hard, motivate yourself to continue by imagining your dream life. Picture how it feels when you've finally hit your goals.

DON'T FORGET

Imagining your dream life, when channeled properly would help you reach it sooner than you expect.

MEDITATE

_____

_____

_____

_____

_____

_____

_____

_____

_____

_____

_____

_____

_____

_____

_____

_____

_____

_____

_____

_____

_____

_____

_____

_____

_____

_____

Dream it until you achieve it!!!

DAY 7

INSIGHT

Having hope in God no matter what life throws at you makes you invincible because you've now rooted yourself in him (God). Never forget that he is the master planner, preparing something big for you.

WHAT YOU SHOULD IMBIBE TODAY

Build yourself to hope and trust in God no matter how heavy the storms around you gets.

<u>DON'T FORGET</u>

God is the alpha and omega, he can
always make a way where there
seems to be no way!!!

MEDITATE

_____

_____

_____

_____

_____

_____

_____

_____

_____

_____

_____

_____

_____

_____

_____

_____

_____

_____

_____

_____

_____

_____

_____

_____

_____

_____

_____

God is wisdom, when you remember him, you shouldn't doubt the process.

YOU'VE FINISHED WITHTHIS ONE WEEK GUIDE. KEEP UP WITH IT.

POSITIVE RESULT COMES WITH IT.

Show Love to people by giving them copies of this.

_____

_____

_____

_____

_____

_____

_____

_____

_____

_____

_____

_____

_____

_____

_____

BYE!

Each time you're deviating, return to this!

74724880R00022